# How to Research Farm History for Metal Detecting

David Villanueva

# DEDICATION

To Helen.

# CONTENTS

1    How to Research Farm History for Metal Detecting    1

2    Treasure Law and Advice for Finders           18

3    Books In Print From The Same Author          28

# 1 HOW TO RESEARCH FARM HISTORY FOR METAL DETECTING

I have said it before and I'll say it again: if you search land where nothing much happened in the past then your finds bag will contain nothing much! So when I was offered the chance to search a farm in the neighbouring county of Sussex, UK, I heeded my own words and knuckled down to some serious research. I have shelves full of books and draws full of maps covering my own county of Kent but on foreign soil, as it were, I had little information. Where do you start? Start at the present time with what is already known or rumoured.

The farm manager told me the farmhouse was a former manor house dating back to the 13th century; there was a 16th century oast house and ancient watermill adjacent to the land, which was crossed by the pilgrims' way. All interesting stuff but it is wise to verify what you are told, while not arguing with your host, of course.

**Gold Tudor iconographic finger-ring from a manor site**

Apparently the previous landowner greeted visitors with the barrel of a shotgun, so not much historical investigation of the farm had taken place until fairly recently. The current landowner, however, had commissioned an archaeological survey of the house, which dated it back to at least the 15th century, so that was a good start. Looking at the Guide to County Histories in my book: **Site Research** I realized I had a copy of the early 19th century series: **The Beauties of England and Wales** covering Sussex but was disappointed to read that the compilers of the history for the two most relevant parishes had failed to meet the publication deadline! You win some, you lose some!

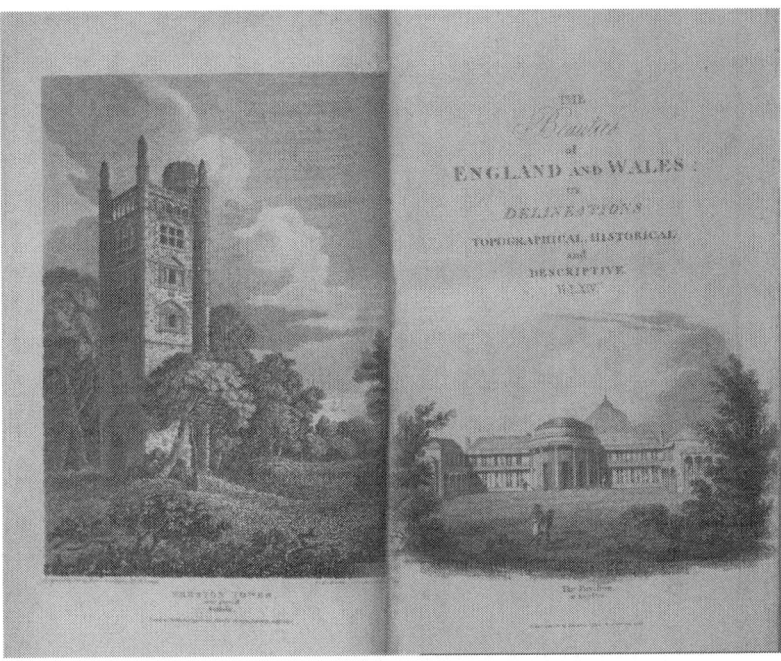

**The Beauties of England and Wales, vol. XIV, Suffolk, Surrey and Sussex, (London, 1813)**

Another tome I have on my shelves is the complete **Domesday Book** (Penguin Books, 2002) covering the entire survey of 34 English Counties. Parish boundaries had changed in this area over time, effectively moving the farm from a declining old parish to an expanding new one. There is no mention of the newer parish in Domesday but the old parish was actually recorded as a hundred in 1086 and possessed one (water) mill.

**Typical water mill**

The Domesday watermill may be the one still standing next door to the farm and clearly there must be a hundred meeting site around somewhere, in fact there is a Hundred House within the parish which is said to be the meeting place.

**Sixth century chip carved button brooch from water mill site**

**Lead papal bulla of Pope Nicholas IV (1288-92) from a Hundred meeting place**

Turning to the Site Guide in my book: **Successful Detecting Sites** I was pleased to discover that the three nearest settlements; north east and west of the farm, which I located on the county map printed in the book, had all held fairs in the past, so there was a good chance that fairgoers had been crossing the farm for several hundred years, sprinkling it with losses.

**George I shilling from a fair site**

With my personal resources exhausted, nearer home I could have popped down to the local library or county archives but here would need a full day out to make it worthwhile. Before making that trip, I decided to see what I could find out on the Internet. If you want to try such research but you are not a computer user, you can easily become one down at your local library.

ARCHI, an acronym derived from archaeological index, is a good place to start. The site http://www.archiuk.com/ lists over 195,000 UK sites ranging from single coin finds to major ancient monuments, its great value from my point of view is that most entries have been gleaned from sources outside metal detecting, so you probably will not find other detectorists already on your chosen site. To perform a quick search you simply enter the relevant UK place, postcode or coordinates click 'search', verify place on the next page and ARCHI UK will return a list of all finds within 10km. If you are not a subscriber you will get a description of the find and a distance from the search point, while subscribers will also get direction, findspot, aerial imagery and maps. If you use ARCHI UK frequently, then the few pounds asked for an annual subscription is time saving and good value for money. As a subscriber, using Advanced Search, I could restrict the search area and had instant access to the findspots otherwise I would have had to Google the site details and hope for the best. A 3km search produced over forty sites, including a Celtic gold coin find, a Roman furnace and a deserted medieval village, so there was plenty of history in the area.

Another on line index or database well worth consulting is the Historic Environment Record (HER): http//www.heritagegateway.org.uk/gateway/chr/ this is the former Sites and Monuments Record (SMR) and tends to concentrate on larger sites than ARCHI such as buildings and earthworks. In some counties Portable Antiquities Scheme (PAS) data for single finds may be included but only to a four figure grid reference. What the HER search did turn up for the parish was a track way of probable prehistoric or Roman date, which ties in nicely with the Roman furnace.

The Ordnance Survey map of Roman Britain did not show this track way, however the foremost authority on Roman roads in Britain was the late Ivan D Margary whose major work was two volumes of **Roman Roads of Britain** published in the 1950s, with the latest edition in 1973. I did have one of Margary's other works, **Roman Ways of the Weald**, which covered this particular track way running very near or perhaps even through the farm.

**Silver Denarius of Antoninus Pius (138-161) from a Roman track way**

An excellent way of finding historical information on the Internet is simply to type into a search engine the name of the county/parish/town/village followed by 'history' and see what turns up. Sussex top spot on Google was 'Sussex History − A Free online history library' with some useful old publications included but a similar search on the parish name produced much better results. The top position was 'The Weald of Kent, Surrey and Sussex', which held a vast database of historical information: books, documents, photographs and, very importantly, maps. In fact there was a range of downloadable maps from John Speed, 1610 to Ordnance Survey, 6 inch to 1 mile, 1899.

Although the relevant pages of the listed sources had been digitised and could be accessed from the site, in some cases the information was incomplete so I thought it would be a good idea to try and obtain more complete sources. A vast number of old publications have been made available for free reading and free download in the last few years. Two sites I find invaluable for gaining access to this mine of information are: Google Books http://books.google.com/ and Internet Archive: http://archive.org/ I use the two because what I can't find on one site I can often find on the other. I managed to find and download both volumes of: **A Compendious History of Sussex** by Mark Antony Lower (1870), which not only gave a good historical description of parishes I was interested in but also indexed the first twenty volumes of the **Sussex**

**Archaeological Collections,** the journal of the Sussex Archaeological Society formed in 1848. Many of these old journals were also available for reading and download on the two sites, so I was able to follow up some of the references.

Another invaluable resource from Google is Google Earth: https://www.google.co.uk/intl/en_uk/earth free software showing aerial views of the entire planet. The major benefit of looking at aerial photographs is that they may show crop marks caused by buried features producing differential growing rates. Crop mark hunting has been made even easier on Google Earth now as you can turn back the clock and view a number of different surveys made during the last dozen years or so. To use the feature, click on the clock icon on the tool bar to reveal the time slider. Although Google Earth allows you to print the aerial photo it doesn't provide much in the way of editing facilities and you can end up with quite a small print. To get around this you can hit the Print Screen button on your keyboard, which copies the current screen onto the clipboard, then paste into MS Paint or a photo editor where you can edit the picture and print from there.

The tithe or enclosure map really is a must for farm history research as it documents every single field and plot of land in many parishes at a very large scale. Tithe maps came about from The Tithe Commutation Act of 1836, whereby the Church's 10% tax on annual produce from the land was commuted from goods to cash, necessitating a very detailed record of the land and its use. The parish I was looking at was covered by a tithe map; however some parishes never had such a map, often this is because their tithes had already been commuted by an earlier enclosure act, in which case the enclosure award and map could just as usefully be studied.

Fields and plots of land on both tithe maps and enclosure maps are numbered and refer to the separate apportionment in the case of tithe maps and award in the case of enclosure maps. Unfortunately only a few tithe or enclosure maps are available online at present. You can do a Google search for tithe maps plus name of county or contact the local library, county archives or The National Archives. The National Archives has a guide here: https://www.nationalarchives.gov.uk/help-with-your-research/research-guides/tithes/

Through a Google search, I discovered that Sussex had put its tithe maps on CD, which could be viewed at certain libraries or purchased for a few pounds for use on a PC at home. Some apportionments, which are absolutely essential for interpreting the map, were also available on CD or by email.

Having tracked down the tithe or enclosure map and corresponding apportionment or award, what use can you make of them? There are several great uses:

* Once enclosure got under way, fields were named so illiterate agricultural workers in the past could easily navigate the landscape at their master's bidding, without the need of maps or complex instructions. The field names often refer to vanished buildings or routes, meeting or trading places, sporting events and other activities that were guaranteed to put metallic losses in the ground. So by studying these field names, productive sites will be found. The names of trading and meeting sites are discussed in my book, **Successful Detecting Sites,** and others will be found analysed in the relevant county volumes published by The English Place-Name Society.

* If you have picked up a lead from elsewhere describing a feature, event or find in a particular named field and need to find the actual field, the map will probably reveal all.

* The state of cultivation of fields recorded in the apportionment can guide you to the probable site of an event. A fair that was held at the time of the survey, for instance, would most likely take place on grassland rather than an arable field.

* The map itself shows field boundaries, buildings, tracks and footpaths as they were nearly 200 years ago, which you can compare to a modern map and highlight the changes.

I ordered the tithe map and apportionment, covering the farm, to be delivered, rather than spend valuable detecting time and money visiting the archives. Based on what I have discovered so far the hot spots are likely to be all searchable land around the main house, all routes across the site and the frontage along the river.

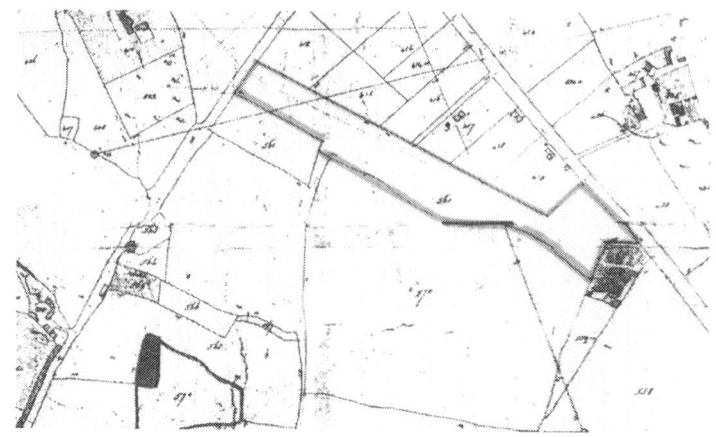

**Part of tithe map showing field where a biannual running race was held
(The National Archives IR30/17/85)**

| LANDOWNERS | OCCUPIERS | NUMBERS REFERRING TO PLAN | NAME AND DESCRIPTION OF LANDS AND PREMISES | STATE OF CULTIVATION | QUANTITIES OF STATUTE MEASURE | | | PAYABLE TO VICAR | | | PAYABLE TO Fagg Sir John Bt Impropriator | | | REMARKS |
|---|---|---|---|---|---|---|---|---|---|---|---|---|---|---|
| | | | | | ACRES | RODS | PERCHES | £ | s | d | £ | s | d | |
| Wildman James Beckford Esq | Taylor Richard | 560 | Running Field | Pasture | 4 | 2 | 3 | | | | | | | |

**Extract from apportionment referring to field (The National Archives
IR29/17/85)**

**A few of the coins found in the *Running Field***

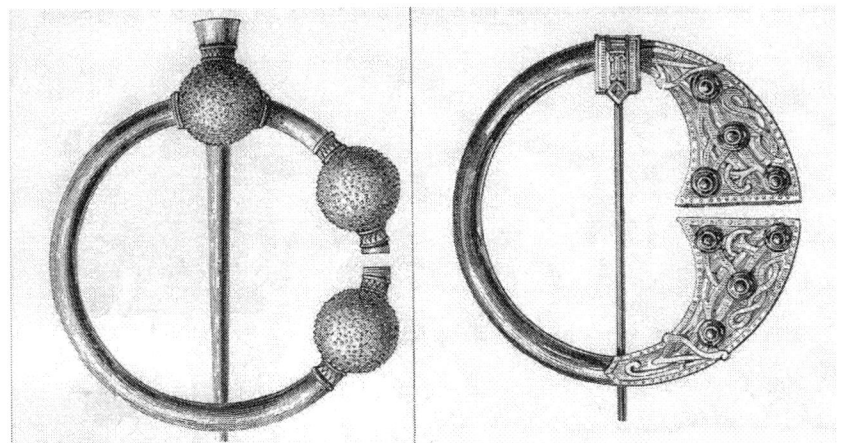

**The Penrith hoard of Viking silver brooches, like these, were found in *Silver field***

# 2 TREASURE LAW AND ADVICE FOR FINDERS

I am sure many readers will be experienced metal detectorists aware of the rules and laws relating to the hobby in Britain. Nevertheless, I have reproduced below, the latest code of practice for metal detecting in England and Wales. The code is generally applicable to the rest of the UK, although governing bodies differ and alternative rules on treasure may apply.

## Code of Practice for Responsible Metal Detecting in England & Wales (2017 Revision)

If undertaken responsibly metal-detecting can make an important contribution to archaeological knowledge. This document aims to provide guidance for metal-detectorists who wish to contribute to our understanding of the history of England and Wales. It combines both the requirements of finders under the law, as well as more general voluntary guidance on accepted best practice.

## Being responsible means:

### Before you go metal-detecting

1. Not trespassing; before you start detecting obtain permission to search from the landowner, regardless of the status, or perceived status, of the land. Remember that all land (including parks, public open-spaces, beaches and foreshores) has an owner and an occupier (such as a tenant farmer) can only grant permission with both the landowner's and tenant's

agreement. Any finds discovered will normally be the property of the landowner, so to avoid disputes it is advisable to get permission and agreement in writing first regarding the ownership of any finds subsequently discovered.

2. Obeying the law concerning protected sites (such as those defined as Scheduled Monuments, Sites of Special Scientific Interest or military crash sites, and those involving human remains), and also those other sites on which metal-detecting might also be restricted (such as land under Countryside Stewardship or other agri-environment schemes). You can obtain details of these sites from several sources, including the landowner/ occupier, your local Finds Liaison Officer or Historic Environment Record or at http://www.magic.gov.uk / https://historicengland.org.uk/listing/the-list/ http://www.cadw.gov.wales — which will help research and better understand the site. Take extra care when detecting near protected sites since it is not always clear where the boundaries of these lie on the ground.

3. Familiarising yourself with the Portable Antiquities Scheme (including contact details for your local Finds Liaison Officer — see https://finds.org.uk / 0207 323 8611), and its guidance on the recording of archaeological finds discovered by the public; make it clear to the landowner that you wish to record finds with the Portable Antiquities Scheme. Ensure that you follow current conservation advice on the handling, care and storage of archaeological objects (https://finds.org.uk/conservation/index).

4. Obtaining public liability insurance (to protect yourself and others from accidental damage), such as that offered by the National Council for Metal Detecting or the Federation of Independent Detectorists.

**While you are metal-detecting**

5. Working on ground that has already been disturbed (such as ploughed land or that which has formerly been ploughed), and only within the depth of ploughing. If detecting takes place on pasture, be careful to ensure that no damage is done to the archaeological value of the land, including earthworks. Avoid damaging stratified archaeological deposits (that is to say, finds that seem to be in the place where they were deposited in antiquity) and minimise any ground disturbance through the

use of suitable tools and by reinstating any ground and turf as neatly as possible.

6. Stopping any digging and making the landowner aware that you are seeking expert help if you discover something below the ploughsoil, or a concentration of finds or unusual material, or wreck remains. Your local Finds Liaison Officer may be able to help or will be able to advise on an appropriate person. Reporting the find does not change your rights of discovery, but will result in far more archaeological evidence being recovered.

7. Recording findspots as accurately as possible for all archaeological finds (i.e. to at least a one ten metre square — an 8-Figure National Grid Reference), using a hand-held Global Positioning Systems (GPS) device whilst in the field or a 1:25000 scale map if this is not possible. Bag finds individually, recording the National Grid Reference on the bag with a waterproof/indelible marker. Archaeologists are interested in learning about all archaeological finds you discover, not just metallic items, because such finds contribute to knowledge.

8. Respecting the Country Code (leave gates and property as you find them and do not damage crops, frighten animals, or disturb ground nesting birds, and dispose properly of litter: see https://www.gov.uk/government/publications/the-countryside-code (You may also like to get a copy of the more extensive Out in the country booklet from Natural England:

http://publications.naturalengland.org.uk/publication/79046)

**After you have been metal-detecting**

9. Reporting all archaeological finds to the relevant landowner/occupier; and making it clear to the landowner that you wish to record archaeological finds to the Portable Antiquities Scheme, so the information can pass into the local Historic Environment Record. Both the Country Land and Business Association and the National Farmers Union support the reporting of finds with the Portable Antiquities Scheme. Details of your local Finds Liaison Officer can be found at see https://finds.org.uk/contacts / e-mail info@finds.org.uk or phone 0207 323 8611.

10. Abiding by the statutory provisions of the Treasure Act 1996, the Treasure Act Code of Practice https://finds.org.uk/treasure and wreck law https://www.gov.uk/government/organisations/maritime-and-coastguard-agency If you wish to take artefacts and archaeological material older than 50 years old out of the UK, you will require an export licence http://www.artscouncil.org.uk/export-controls/export-licensing If you need advice your local Finds Liaison Officer will be able to help you.

11. Calling the Police (101), and notifying the landowner/occupier, if you find any traces of human remains or a likely burial; human remains can only be disturbed further with a Ministry of Justice licence https://www.gov.uk/apply-for-an-exhumation-licence

12. Calling the Police or HM Coastguard, and notifying the landowner/occupier, if you find anything that may be a live explosive, device or other ordnance. Do not attempt to move or interfere with any such explosives.

13. Calling the Police if you notice any illegal activity whilst out metal-detecting, such as theft of farm equipment or illegal metal-detecting (nighthawking). Further details can be found by contacting Historic England/Cadw or the 'heritage crime' contact within your local police force.

While I do not pretend to be a lawyer, there are a number of legal definitions that could apply to metal detecting finds together with the popular court ruling on finds made under each category:

**Lost property**, which has been involuntarily parted from its owner, belongs to the owner or their heirs and if they cannot be traced, title goes to the finder. You are legally obliged to take reasonable steps to return lost property to its owner. In the case of loose change it is highly unlikely you will find an owner, so that is yours to keep. Recently a woman received a fine and a criminal record for theft because she found and kept a £20 note on the floor of a shop. If you find a large sum of money or a piece of jewelry, for example, you could report it to the local police, if lost property is in their remit, or take suitable action to find the owner such as advertising in a local newspaper or on social media. The police generally disclaim lost property after one month. Although recently, as the police do not have a statutory duty to deal with lost property, some forces are no longer accepting lost property so, as long as you can show you have made reasonable attempts to trace the owner, it is yours to keep unless it may be evidence of a crime, is dangerous, illegal (e.g. an offensive weapon) or contains personal information. Reasonable steps to trace the owner today usually involve social media such as neighbourhood groups and providing you do that and wait a month or so, the find is technically yours. Bear in mind that the owner retains all rights to their property, so if he or she turns up later then they can still legally demand its return or all proceeds if the item has been sold. The owner may offer you a reward for returning their property but is under no obligation to do so and you would be committing an offence if you refuse to hand the property back unless a reward is paid. The joy expressed when you hand back lost jewelry is reward enough in itself. In Britain, if you find paper money which is unfit for circulation, the Bank of England will usually be able to replace it. Take any banknotes to your local bank in the first instance for advice.

**Mislaid property**, where the owner puts the object down and forgets about it, reverts to the site owner, if not claimed by the owner.

**Abandoned property**, which is simply thrown away, goes to the finder.

**Embedded property** refers to buried artefacts or even natural minerals, which fall outside the definition of treasure trove. Court rulings for such finds will generally be the same as for treasure trove.

**Archaeological objects or portable antiquities** may cover excavated objects as recent as 50 years old. Except for treasure items, reporting in the UK is only mandatory in Scotland, where a reward is paid for retained items. Voluntary reporting is encouraged in the rest of the UK for non-treasure items. Export licenses may be required before such objects can be removed from the country.

**Treasure trove**, defined as objects, less than 300 years old, made substantially of gold, silver and their alloys (plus paper money) hidden or concealed for several decades, with the intention of recovery, where the owners or heirs cannot be traced. Treasure trove is now incorporated in the Treasure Act in England and Wales, although paper money is excluded. Treasure is normally shared equally between land or site owner and finder. If the finder was trespassing then finds go to the landowner or site owner. Finds on government land go to the government unless there is a prior agreement in place.

**Wreck**, being an abandoned vessel (including aircraft), or something abandoned off a vessel, which is afloat, stranded, aground or sunken. The salvager is normally entitled to a reward related to the value of the find. Wreck that we find, for the most part, will be washed up or buried on a beach. Deciding what is wreck is mainly a matter of common sense but if you are unsure, contact your Finds Liaison Officer for advice or report it anyway. Further information is available from: https://www.gov.uk/guidance/wreck-and-salvage-law

## The Treasure Act in Britain

At present, treasure is defined, under the Act, as any object other than a coin, at least 300 years old when found, which has a metallic content, of which at least 10% by weight is gold or silver. And all coins that contain at least 10% by weight of gold or silver that come from the same find consisting of at least two coins, at least 300 years old. And all coins that contain less than 10% by weight gold or silver that come from the same find consisting of at least ten coins at least 300 years old. And any associated objects, except un-worked natural objects (e.g. a pot or other container), found in the same place as treasure objects. And any objects or coin hoards less than 300 years old, made substantially of gold and silver that have been deliberately hidden with the intention of recovery and for which the owner is unknown. Since 1 January 2003 the definition of treasure has been extended on prehistoric (i.e. up to the end of the Iron Age) finds to include all multiple artifacts, made of any metal, found together and single artifacts deliberately containing any quantity of precious metal.

The Act applies to objects found anywhere in England, Wales and Northern Ireland, including in or on land, in buildings (whether occupied or ruined), in rivers and lakes and on the foreshore (the area between mean high water and mean low water) providing the object does not come from a wreck.

If you are searching in other parts of the British Isles or outside of Britain altogether, you should familiarize yourself with treasure law and the laws on metal detecting, for your specific area. In Scotland, for instance, all ownerless objects belong to the Crown. They must be reported regardless of where they were found or of what they are made. The finder receives market value as long as no laws have been broken. Not all finds will be claimed. Further information from: Treasure Trove Unit, National Museum of Scotland, Chambers Street, Edinburgh, EH1 1JF.

I have the experience of having had to report over a dozen separate finds of treasure since the introduction of the Treasure Act. While there were concerns over lack of confidentiality regarding the find spot in the early days, everything has settled down, generally working well and fairly to all parties involved. I still urge you to be cautious when reporting your finds, so here are my unofficial suggestions for protecting yourself and your landowner friends when you find potential treasure:

* Leave your treasure 'as found' and resist all temptation to clean or restore your find except for the absolute minimum necessary to identify it as possible treasure.

* The National Council for Metal Detecting will willingly advise in the process of reporting treasure and it is well worth involving them from the start when you have possible treasure to report.

* County Finds Liaison Officers (FLOs) are now heavily involved in the

treasure process and will also advise and help.

* Your only legal obligation is to report the finding of potential treasure to the Coroner within fourteen days of becoming aware that it is possibly treasure.

* Discuss the matter with the landowner as soon as possible.

* Do the reporting yourself. The legal responsibility for reporting rests with the finder and no one will look after your interests as well as you.

* Bear in mind, especially if you want to keep the coin, that the first coin found of a scattered hoard may not be treasure, if it was the only coin found on that occasion and there was sufficient time to sell the coin before the finding of the second coin.

* Report your find to the Coroner in writing within 14 days and keep a copy of the letter. In the first instance only report the find spot as the name of the parish in which the find was made. If it is not clear which Coroner needs to be informed, ask your FLO or write to the most likely Coroner and ask for your letter to be passed on, as necessary. In my area it is current practice for finds to be reported to the FLO in lieu of the Coroner. As this is not strictly the letter of the law, I report to the Coroner in writing and send a copy to the FLO.

* Always take photographs or have photographs taken of all possible views of all objects, before you hand the objects over. You will at least have something to show an independent valuation expert and, if you want to publish, there will not be any copyright or access issues.

* There is no time limit for handing over the find and you should be allowed a reasonable amount of time for such things as photographing, valuing, showing it to the landowner, displaying it at a club meeting etc. Bear in mind, however, that you are responsible for the security of the find until you hand it over.

* These days Finds Liaison Officers often collect potential treasure from finders; however you may be asked to deposit your find at a museum or FLO at your own expense. You are not legally obliged to take your find anywhere, however, if you can arrange this it is best to comply. Insist on being given the Treasure Receipt, (filled out in your presence) in

exchange for your find.

* The Treasure Act Code of Practice requires that the precise find spot must be established and should be kept confidential. You can <u>insist</u> on the confidentiality requirement when the Treasure Receipt is completed and have the precise find spot kept separately.

* A section of the Treasure Receipt is labeled 'Location of find spot'. Only enter vague details of the find spot such as name of Parish, four-figure map reference or a nondescript site name such as 'Field A'.

* If a museum is interested in acquiring the find, a Coroner's Inquest will be arranged. You should be invited to attend the Inquest for which you can claim expenses and I suggest you should attend if you possibly can – you will at least know who was there and what was said. The press may be there, so be careful not to reveal find spot information if they are.

* Following an Inquest the Press will probably want to speak to you. Whether you speak to them is up to you but you can at least appeal for some confidentiality and perhaps avoid them uncovering, or inventing, more than you would like revealed.

* The final stumbling block is the valuation, which will be given via the Department for Culture Media and Sport some weeks after the Inquest. You need to know if the valuation is 'A Fair Market Value' so that you can decide whether to accept it. Fair market value is an attempt to arrive at the price you should expect to get if selling your find on the open market and the Treasure Valuation Committee tries to arrive at the 'hammer' price without auctioneer's deductions. Pick out a couple of dealers specializing in coins or objects similar to yours from the advertisements in treasure hunting magazines. Ask the dealers to give you their buying-in price for your find (send photographs if necessary). I am sure they will oblige for little or no charge. If the treasure is very rare it should be possible to arrange viewing for independent appraisal. You should be offered two opportunities to contest the valuation, one before the valuation committee meets and one after. I would accept the valuation if it falls within or above your dealers' ballpark figures and contest it if it falls below. If you are going to contest the valuation, get in before the committee meets if you can. There is a slight possibility that the museum involved may contest the valuation and succeed in getting it

reduced – if this happens, unless there is clear justification, you could appeal against it all the way to the Secretary of State, if necessary.

* An alternative is for you or the landowner or both to refuse any award for the find when you first report it or at any time, preferably prior to any inquest. The find will then be offered to interested museums at a 50% or 100% discount depending, if one or both parties refuse the award.

###

# 3 BOOKS IN PRINT FROM THE SAME AUTHOR

THE SUCCESSFUL TREASURE HUNTER'S SECRET
MANUAL: Discovering Treasure Auras in the Digital Age,
Soft Cover, 230mm x 150mm, (9 x 6 inches) 97 pages,
(CSIP, 2016), ISBN 978 1540747815

(Also an E-Book under the title: THE SUCCESSFUL TREASURE
HUNTER'S SECRET MANUAL: How to Use Modern
Cameras to Locate Buried Metals, Gold, Silver, Coins,
Caches…)

CLEANING COINS & ARTEFACTS: Conservation * Restoration
* Presentation, Soft Cover, 210mm x 146mm, (8.25 x 5.75
inches) 110 pages, (Greenlight Publishing, 2008) ISBN 978
1 897738 337

(Also an E-Book under the title: THE SUCCESSFUL TREASURE
HUNTER'S ESSENTIAL COIN AND RELIC
MANAGER: How to Clean, Conserve, Display,
Photograph, Repair, Restore, Replicate and Store Metal
Detecting Finds)

PERMISSION IMPOSSIBLE: Metal Detecting Search Permission
Made Easy, Soft Cover, 210mm x 146mm, (8.25 x 5.75
inches) 78 pages, (True Treasure Books, 2007) ISBN 978 0

9550325 3 0 (Also an E-Book)

SITE RESEARCH FOR DETECTORISTS, FIELDWALKERS & ARCHAEOLOGISTS, Soft Cover, 250mm x 190mm, (9.75 x 7.5 inches) 160 pages, (Greenlight Publishing, 2006) ISBN 1 897738 285

SUCCESSFUL DETECTING SITES: Locate 1000s of Superb Sites and Make More Finds, Soft Cover, 250mm x 190mm, (9.75 x 7.5 inches) 238 pages, (Greenlight Publishing, 2007) ISBN 978 1 897738 306

THE SUCCESSFUL TREASURE HUNTER'S ESSENTIAL SITE RESEARCH MANUAL: How to Find Productive Metal Detecting Sites, (E-Book)

THE ESSENTIAL GUIDE TO OLD, ANTIQUE AND ANCIENT METAL SPOONS, Soft Cover, 210mm x 146mm, 88 pages, (True Treasure Books, 2008) ISBN 978 0 9550325 4 7 (Also an E-Book)

DOWSING FOR TREASURE: The New Successful Treasure Hunter's Essential Dowsing Manual, Soft Cover, 230mm x 150mm, (9 x 6 inches) 96 pages, (CSIP, 2016) ISBN 978-1518766060 (Also an E-Book)

MY ANCESTOR LEFT AN HEIRLOOM: Discovering Heirlooms and Ancestors Through the Metalwork They Left Behind, Soft Cover, 210mm x 146mm, (8.25 x 5.75 inches) 84 pages, (True Treasure Books, 2011) ISBN 978 0 9550325 6 1

(Also an E-Book under the title: MY ANCESTOR LEFT AN HEIRLOOM: Hunting Family History and Genealogy Treasure Through Metal Detecting Finds)

METAL DETECTING MADE EASY: A Guide for Beginners and Reference for All, Soft Cover, 210mm x 146mm, (8.25 x 5.75 inches) 128 pages, (True Treasure Books, 2014) ISBN

978 0 9550325 7 8 (Also an E-Book)

FAITHFUL ATTRACTION: How to Drive Your Metal Detector to Find Treasure (E-Book)

TOKENS & TRADERS OF KENT in the Seventeenth, Eighteenth & Nineteenth Centuries, Soft Cover, 215mm x 140mm, (8.5 x 5.5 inches) 112 pages, (True Treasure Books, 2015) ISBN 978 0 9550325 8 5 (Also an E-Book)

HOW TO FIND BRITAIN'S BURIED TREASURE HOARDS, Soft Cover, 295mm x 210mm, (11.75 x 8.25 inches) 150 pages, (Greenlight Publishing, 2017) ISBN 978 1 897738 627

METAL DETECTING BENEFITS FOR LANDOWNERS, (with Jacq le Breton), Soft Cover, 230mm x 150mm, (9 x 6 inches) 28 pages, (CSIP, 2016) ISBN 978-1537341118 (Put your contact details on the back cover and give to landowners when requesting permission)

TREASURE HUNTING for PROFIT: With and Without a Metal Detector, Soft Cover, 230mm x 150mm, (9 x 6 inches) 220 pages, (CSIP, 2018), ISBN 978 1726407847 (Also an E-Book)

GUIDE TO WHITSTABLE AND ITS SURROUNDINGS 1876 (Illustrated), (W J Cox) Soft Cover, 230mm x 150mm, (9 x 6 inches) 103 pages, (Independently Published, 2019), ISBN 9781794180987 (Also an E-Book)

MANOR HOUSES OF BEDFORDSHIRE PAST AND PRESENT, Soft Cover, 230mm x 150mm, (9 x 6 inches) 102 pages, (Independently Published, 2019), ISBN 9781075574238 (Also an E-Book)

INTERNET SITE RESEARCH FOR DETECTORISTS: How to Find Productive UK Metal Detecting Sites Using the World Wide Web, Soft Cover, 230mm x 150mm, (9 x 6 inches) 75 pages, (Independently Published, 2019), ISBN 9781693198311 (Also an E-Book)

THE SUCCESSFUL METAL DETECTORIST'S SITE AND FINDS LOG BOOK, Soft Cover, 230mm x 150mm, (9 x 6 inches) 249 pages, (Independently Published, 2019), ISBN 9781705335918

A GUIDE TO EUROPEAN COINS 800 BC - 1900 AD, Soft Cover, 230mm x 150mm, (9 x 6 inches) 174 pages, (Independently Published, 2020), ISBN 9798666302606 (Also an E-Book)

THE SUCCESSFUL METAL DETECTING SITE AND FINDS LOG BOOK, Soft Cover, 230mm x 150mm, (9 x 6 inches) 133 pages, (Independently Published, 2020), ISBN 9798669425456

THE SUCCESSFUL METAL DETECTING SITE LOG BOOK, Soft Cover, 230mm x 150mm, (9 x 6 inches) 131 pages, (Independently Published, 2020), ISBN 9798669891527

THE SUCCESSFUL METAL DETECTING FINDS LOG BOOK, Soft Cover, 230mm x 150mm, (9 x 6 inches) 131 pages, (Independently Published, 2020), ISBN 9798669919368

HOW TO RESEARCH FARM HISTORY FOR METAL DETECTING (E-Book, 2020)

METAL DETECTING BRONZE AGE BRITAIN (E-Book, 2021)

METAL DETECTING IRON AGE BRITAIN (E-Book, 2021)

METAL DETECTING ROMAN BRITAIN (E-Book, 2021)

METAL DETECTING ANGLO-SAXON & VIKING BRITAIN (E-Book, 2021)

Books are available from True Treasure Books online at

http://www.truetreasurebooks.net and your favourite online and offline retailers.

# ABOUT THE AUTHOR

David Villanueva was born in Birmingham, England in 1951. In 1972 his mother bought him Ted Fletcher's book, **A Fortune Under Your Feet**, which inspired him to buy a BFO metal detector. The performance was poor by current standards but it found coins and David became hooked.

In 1985, a move to Kent, England saw David searching beaches with an old Pulse Induction detector. The machine's sensitivity to iron and zero discrimination did not suit local conditions, so he bought a new Induction Balance detector, which worked well on the dry beaches and encouraged him to try inland sites. He joined a metal detecting club and gained permission to search a small farm, making all manner of old and interesting finds. Having a keen interest in history, David researched his locality, which led to more productive sites to search and write about in over a dozen books and the two British metal detecting magazines – **Treasure Hunting** and **The Searcher** – which have published more than two dozens of David's articles.

But it was a chance encounter with Britain's best treasure dowser, Jimmy Longton that supercharged David's treasure hunting. Jimmy, who had dowsed his way to a $60,000 Viking silver hoard, taught David how to dowse for treasure with remarkable results. David suddenly found himself reporting real treasures in the form of caches of ancient tools and gold coins as well as Roman, Saxon and medieval gold and silver jewelry. David has recorded many finds under the Treasure Act and continually holds trophies won at the Swale Search and Recovery Club, which he now chairs.

Connect with me online: http://www.truetreasurebooks.net

Made in the USA
Columbia, SC
27 November 2023